Secrets T   t
Want)
7 Simpl

&

Avoiding a Debt Sentence

America's #1 Source for Credit Secrets Today

Author of *Secrets of a Deal'ionaire, Creating Wealth One Small Deal at a Time* and *How to Improve Your Credit Score*

© HHLLC 2015. Secrets *THOSE* Credit Doctors Don't Want *YOU* to Know. Deal'ionaire OTC System *Signature* Series. All Rights Reserved

Secrets *THOSE* Credit Doctors Don't Want *YOU* to Know ~ *Work Book*
7 *Simple Steps* to a Higher Credit Score

&

Avoiding a *Debt Sentence*

This information may not be reproduced, copied, stored in a retrieval system, recorded by video, audio, scanned, photographed, transmitted in whole or part, in any form by any means, electronic, mechanical, photocopying, recording or otherwise shared in any way whatsoever without written permission of the owner under penalty of law and remains the sole property of the owner.

This information is intended for illustration purposes only. Actual financial impact may vary as it may be affected by additional factors not considered in this information. The results generated by the strategies, methods, or techniques described in this information should not be used for any planning, forecasting or any other similar business purposes.

The information is provided "AS IS" without warranty of any kind, express or implied, and in no event shall the owner be liable for any damages whatsoever in relation with the use of this information. The participant agrees to indemnify and hold harmless, and waive any liabilities or claims against the owner that result from this information.

Confidential — Non-Transferable Licensed Material © 2015 HHLLC. Secrets *THOSE* Credit Doctors Don't Want *YOU* to Know. Deal'ionaire OTC System *Signature* Series. All Rights Reserved

Secrets *THOSE* Credit Doctors Don't Want *YOU* to Know ~ *Work Book*
7 *Simple Steps* to a Higher Credit Score

&

Avoiding a *Debt Sentence*

Secrets *THOSE* Credit Doctors Don't Want *YOU* to Know ~ <u>*Work Book*</u>
7 *Simple Steps* to a Higher Credit Score

&

Avoiding a Debt Sentence

Table of Contents

Secrets *THOSE* Credit Doctors Don't Want *YOU* to Know ~ <u>*Work Book*</u>
7 *Simple Steps* to a Higher Credit Score

&

Avoiding a *Debt Sentence*

Why do We Care about Our Credit Scores?

Where do We start?

The first step in determining how to improve your credit score is to start where you are at right now. How do you do this?

Get a copy of your credit report. Where?

A good place to get a *Free* snap shot of your credit report with the score is CreditKarma.com

Score_____ Date_____

Score_____ Date_____

Score_____ Date_____

Score_____ Date_____

Score_____ Date_____

Score_____ Date_____

Score_____ Date_____

Score_____ Date_____

Score_____ Date_____

Score_____ Date_____

Score_____ Date_____

Score_____ Date_____

How Are Scores Calculated?

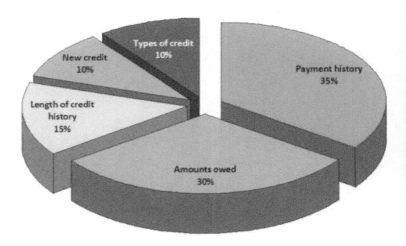

- **35% = Payment History**
- **10% = Types of Credit**
- **10% = Credit Inquiries**
- **15% = Credit History**
- **30% = Amount, i.e. Proportion of Balance to Limits**

Payment History/How Paid = 35%

**Account_____Paid__OnTime_
_30daysLate__60daysLate__90daysLate**

- Account_____Paid__OT__30__60__90

- Account_____Paid__OT__30__60__90

- Account_____Paid__OT__30__60__90

- Account_____Paid__OT__30__60__90

- Account_____Paid__OT__30__60__90

- Account_____Paid__OT__30__60__90

- Account_____Paid__OT__30__60__90

- Account_____Paid__OT__30__60__90

- Account_____Paid__OT__30__60__90

- Account_____Paid__OT__30__60__90

Types Of Accounts = 10%

Account_____Revolving(CC)__Mortgage__Auto __StoreCard__PayDayLoan__Other

Account_____CC__Mort__A__SC__PDL__O

Account_____CC__Mort__A__SC__PDL__O

Account_____CC__Mort__A__SC__PDL__O

Account_____CC__Mort__A__SC__PDL__O

Account_____CC__Mort__A__SC__PDL__O

Account_____CC__Mort__A__SC__PDL__O

Account_____CC__Mort__A__SC__PDL__O

Account_____CC__Mort__A__SC__PDL__O

Account_____CC__Mort__A__SC__PDL__O

Account_____CC__Mort__A__SC__PDL__O

Credit Inquiries = 10%

of Inquiries

Last 6 months_____

Last 12 months_____

Last 24 months_____

Credit History/Age of Accounts = 15%

Account_____Date Opened_____Age_____

Account_____Date Opened_____Age_____

Account_____Date Opened_____Age_____

Account_____Date Opened_____Age_____

Account_____Date Opened_____Age_____

Account_____Date Opened_____Age_____

Account_____Date Opened_____Age_____

Account_____Date Opened_____Age_____

Account_____Date Opened_____Age_____

Account_____Date Opened_____Age_____

Account_____Date Opened_____Age_____

Amount Owed/Proportion of Balance to Limits = 30%

Account_____Balance____Credit Limit_____%____

Account_____Balance_____Credit Limit_____%____

Account_____Balance_____Credit Limit_____%____

Account_____Balance_____Credit Limit_____%____

Account_____Balance_____Credit Limit_____%____

Account_____Balance_____Credit Limit_____%____

Account_____Balance_____Credit Limit_____%____

Account_____Balance_____Credit Limit_____%____

Account_____Balance_____Credit Limit_____%____

Account_____Balance_____Credit Limit_____%____

Account_____Balance_____Credit Limit_____%____

Bankruptcy___Date Filed_____Chapter 11 / 13

Judgments

Date Reported_____Type_____

Collections

Date Reported_____Type_____

Write dispute letters to the credit bureaus

Letters written_____

Date Sent___Response Received_____

Letters written_____

Date Sent___Response Received_____

Letters written_____

Date Sent___Response Received_____

Sample Dispute Letter to Credit Bureaus

April 15, 2015

To Whom It May Concern:

There is some incorrect information on my credit report that needs to be verified and corrected.

J.J. Pennry account number 345987 is not my account and I do not owe them any money. Please verify this information and delete the account when updated. Let me know when the correction has been made.

Thank you.

John Q. Doe
SSN 555-55-5555

123 Main Street
Anytown USA 11111

Don't forget to sign it

Add a Fraud and/or Any Statement

Statement Added___Date Sent____Response Received____

Statement Added___Date Sent____Response Received____

Statement Added___Date Sent____Response Received____

Sample Fraud Statement

Sample Fraud Statement to Add to Your
Credit Report

April 15, 2015

To Whom It May Concern:

Due to Identity theft concerns please add the
following Fraud Statement to my credit report:

Do Not extend credit to anyone using my name and
social security number without first obtaining a
government issued picture I.D. and calling me on my
personal phone for further verification. You must
also call me @ 123-555-3245.

Thank you.

John Q. Doe
SSN 555-55-5555

123 Main Street
Anytown USA 11111

Don't forget to sign it

Three Major Credit Reporting Bureaus

Experian

701 Experian Parkway
P.O. Box 4500
Allen TX 75013

https://www.experian.com/consumer/upload//

1.888.397.3742

Trans Union

2 Baldwin Place
P.O. Box 1000
Chester PA 19022

https://dispute.transunion.com/dp/dispute/landingPage.jsp

1.800.916.8800

Equifax

P.O. Box 740256
Atlanta, GA 30374

https://www.ai.equifax.com/CreditInvestigation/home.acti
on

1.800.685.1111

*These addresses and phone numbers are current as of publication.
They do change from time to time. It is recommended you verify the
information before corresponding.

SECRETS THOSE CREDIT DOCTORS DON'T WANT YOU TO KNOW

ID Theft and Tax-Return Fraud Concerns

Form 14039 Rev. February 2014	Department of the Treasury - Internal Revenue Service **Identity Theft Affidavit**	OMB Number 1545-2139

Complete and submit this form if you are an actual or potential victim of identity theft and would like the IRS to mark your account to identify questionable activity.

Check only one of the following two boxes if they apply to your specific situation. (Optional for all filers)

☐ I am submitting this form in response to a mailed notice or letter from the IRS.

☐ I am completing this form on behalf of another person, such as a deceased spouse or other deceased relative. You should provide information for the actual or potential victim in Sections A, B, & D.

Note to all filers: Failure to provide required information on BOTH sides of this form AND clear and legible documentation will delay processing.

THIS FORM MUST BE SIGNED ON THE REVERSE SIDE (SECTION F).

Section A – Reason For Filing This Form (Required for all filers)

Check only ONE of the following two boxes. You MUST provide the requested description or explanation in the lined area below.

1 ☐ I am a victim of identity theft AND it is affecting my federal tax records.

You should check this box if, for example, your attempt to file electronically was rejected because someone had already filed using your Social Security Number (SSN) or Individual Taxpayer Identification Number (ITIN), or if you received a notice or correspondence from the IRS indicating someone was otherwise using your number.

Provide a short explanation of the problem and how you were made aware of it.

2 ☐ I have experienced an event involving my personal information that may at some future time affect my federal tax records.

You should check this box if you are the victim of non-federal tax related identity theft, such as the misuse of your personal identity information to obtain credit. You should also check this box if no identity theft violation has occurred, but you have experienced an event that could result in identity theft, such as a lost/stolen purse or wallet, home robbery, etc.

Briefly describe the identity theft violation(s) and/or the event(s) of concern. Include the date(s) of the incident(s).

....
....
....
....
....
....

Section B – Taxpayer Information (Required for all filers)

Taxpayer's last name	First name	Middle initial	The last 4 digits of the taxpayer's SSN or the taxpayer's complete Individual Taxpayer Identification Number (ITIN)

Taxpayer's current mailing address (apt., suite no. and street, or P.O. Box)

City		State	ZIP code

Tax year(s) affected *(Required if you checked Box 1 in Section A above.)* | Last tax return filed (year) *(If you are not required to file a return, enter NRF and do not complete the next two lines.)*

Address on last tax return filed *(If same as current address, write "same as above")*

City (on last tax return filed)		State	ZIP code

Section C – Telephone Contact Information (Required for all filers)

Telephone number *(include area code)* ☐ Home ☐ Work ☐ Cell | Best time(s) to call

I prefer to be contacted in *(select the appropriate language)* ☐ English ☐ Spanish ☐ Other _____

Section D – Required Documentation (Required for all filers)

Submit this completed form and a clear and legible photocopy of at least one of the following documents to verify your identity. If you are submitting this form on behalf of another person, the documentation should be for that person. If necessary, enlarge the photocopies so all information and pictures are clearly visible.

Check the box next to the document(s) you are submitting:

☐ Passport ☐ Drivers license ☐ Social Security Card ☐ Other valid U.S. Federal or State government issued identification**

** Do not submit photocopies of federally issued identification where prohibited by 18 U.S.C. 701 (e.g., official badges designating federal employment).

Form **14039** (Rev. 2-2014) Catalog Number 52525A   www.irs.gov   Department of the Treasury - Internal Revenue Service

41

Form 14039	Department of the Treasury - Internal Revenue Service	OMB Number
Rev. February 2014	**Identity Theft Affidavit**	1545-2139

Section E – Representative Information (Required only if completing this form on someone else's behalf)

If you are completing this form on behalf of another person, you **must** complete this section and attach clear and legible photocopies of the documentation indicated.

Check only **ONE** of the following four boxes next to the reason why you are submitting this form

☐ The taxpayer is deceased and I am the surviving spouse. (No attachments are required)

☐ The taxpayer is deceased and I am the court-appointed or certified personal representative.
Attach a copy of the court certificate showing your appointment.

☐ The taxpayer is deceased and a court-appointed or certified personal representative has not been appointed.
Attach a copy of the death certificate or the formal notification from the appropriate government office informing the next of kin of the decedent's death. Indicate your relationship to the decedent.

☐ The taxpayer is unable to complete this form and I have been appointed conservator or have Power of Attorney (POA) authorization.
Attach a copy of the documentation showing your appointment as conservator or your POA authorization.
If you are the POA and have been issued a CAF number by the IRS, enter it here: _____

Representative's name

Current mailing address

City	State	ZIP code

Section F – Penalty Of Perjury Statement and Signature (Required for all filers)

Under penalty of perjury, I declare that, to the best of my knowledge and belief, the information entered on this form is true, correct, complete, and made in good faith.

Signature of taxpayer or representative of taxpayer	Date signed

Instructions for Submitting this Form

Submit this form and clear and legible copies of required documentation using ONE of the following submission options. Mailing AND faxing this form WILL result in a processing delay.

By Mail	By FAX

Form **14039** (Rev. 2-2014) Catalog Number 52525A   www.irs.gov   Department of the Treasury - Internal Revenue Service

Or go to :

http://www.irs.gov/uac/Tax-Fraud-Alerts

Secured Credit Card sources starting from ZERO & Below

Progress Credit – offers 3 MasterCard's

https://www.progresscredit.com/card_options

Open Sky – offers Visa card

https://www.openskycc.com

OneUnited Bank – offers Visa card

https://www.oneunited.com

First Choice Bank – offers 2 Visa cards

http://www.securedcardchoice.com

Merrick Bank – offers Visa card

https://securedcard.merrickbank.com

USAA Secured Cards – offers MasterCard & American Express card for US veterans

https://www.usaa.com/inet/pages/banking_credit_cards_main?wa_ref=lf_product_bank_cc

Bad Credit – No Credit – Starting from ZERO & Below

Account applied for_____**Date**_____**Response recv'd**_____

Unsecured Cards

Acc_____Date_____Rcv'd_____

Acc_____Date_____Rcv'd_____

Acc_____Date_____Rcv'd_____

Secured Cards

Acc_____Date_____Rcv'd_____

Acc_____Date_____Rcv'd_____

Acc_____Date_____Rcv'd_____

Authorized User Accounts

Acc_____Date_____Rcv'd_____

Acc_____Date_____Rcv'd_____

Acc_____Date_____Rcv'd_____

7 Simple Steps to Higher Credit Score

&

Avoiding a *Debt Sentence*

1) Pay Your Bills – On Time

2) *Don't* necessarily close older and/or paid off accounts

3) *Don't* get unnecessary inquiries

4) *Keep* Balance in Proportion to Limits at 30-40% or less

5) *Dispute* Incorrect information

6) *A*dd a fraud and/or any statement to your credit report

7) *Smile*, Relax & Sleep well tonight

<u>Notes</u>

<u>Notes</u>

Congratulations on Your Wise Decision to Become a VIP in the Deal'ionaire OTC Signature Series. The information is Priceless.

Because of Your VIP Status You are Entitled to Many Special Insider Bonuses. Always check for the up-to-date programs, boot camps, workshops and trainings.

For Opportunities And Qualifications contact us at **TheDealionaire@gmail.com** Use your Special VIP code – *STCDPWB17*

Some of the Current Premier Program Opportunities in Deal'ionaire OTC *Signature Series** include:

Boot Camp-Intensive-

*Secrets of a Deal'ionaire Creating Wealth One Small Deal at a Time
Bonus $400 to $4,400 in 40 days

Workshop-

*Wholesaling Real Estate Today"
No Money
No Credit
No Problem

Trainings

*Secrets THOSE Credit Doctors Don't
Want YOU to Know
Bonus 7 Simple Steps to a Higher Credit
Score
and
Avoiding a Debt Sentence

*Turning Renters Into Buyers
5 Simple Steps to Turn Your Renters into
Buyers

● *Check often for Opportunities and
Availability There is often a Waiting List*

For further Self Study be sure to get Your Own copy of my other books.

On Amazon.com

How to Improve Your Credit Score

What Everyone Needs to Know

John R Lee

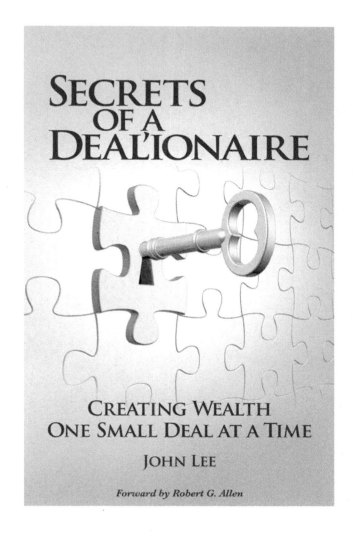

Stay in Touch:

Facebook =
www.facebook.com/MillionairesRUS

Twitter =
https://twitter.com/johnLeeFromMO

What's New =
www.millionairesrus.blogspot.com

Email = **TheDealionaire@gmail.com**

This Coupon Entitles Bearer to
ONE FREE HUG
Redeemable Anytime

Confidential — Non-Transferable Licensed Material

© HHLLC 2015. Secrets *THOSE* Credit Doctors Don't Want *YOU* to Know.
Deal'ionaire OTC System *Signature* Series. All Rights Reserved

Special Bonus Just for *YOU*

4 Easy Steps to Prevent ID Theft And IRS Tax Refund Theft

Special VIP Deal'ionaire BONUS

~ FREE for You a $197 Value ~

Send Request to   STCDPWB117 at
TheDealionaire@gmail.com

Confidential — Non-Transferable Licensed Material

© HHLLC 2015. Secrets *THOSE* Credit Doctors Don't Want *YOU* to Know. Deal'ionaire OTC System *Signature* Series. All Rights Reserved

CREDIT SCORE
720-850
700-719
675-699
620-674
560-619
500-559

Confidential — Non-Transferable Licensed Material

© HHLLC 2015. Secrets *THOSE* Credit Doctors Don't Want *YOU* to Know.
Deal'ionaire OTC System *Signature* Series. All Rights Reserved.

Secrets *THOSE* Credit Doctors Don't Want *YOU* to Know

7 *Simple Steps* to a Higher Credit Score
&
Avoiding a *Debt Sentence*

Confidential — Non-Transferable Licensed Material

**© HHLLC 2015. Secrets *THOSE* Credit Doctors Don't Want *YOU* to Know.
Deal'ionaire OTC System *Signature* Series. All Rights Reserved.**